How to Publish a Book

Your Complete Guide on How to Self Publish a Kindle and Paperback Book on Amazon

By Rob Branson

Copyright© 2019
All Rights Reserved
ISBN: 9798607424787
Published by ZML Corp LLC

Table of Contents

Disclaimer 3

About the Author 5

Introduction 7

Part 1A: Making Your Book 9

Part 1B: Kindle Create 15

Part 1C: Publishing Your Kindle Book 25

Part 2A: Making Your Paperback Book 33

Part 2B: Publishing Your Paperback Book 41

Part 3: Linking the Kindle and Paperback Book .. 49

Conclusion 51

Disclaimer

This book is written for informational and entertainment purposes only. None of this book should be considered legal or personal advice. Copyright © 2019, all rights reserved. None of this book can be reproduced or copied without written consent from the author or publisher. Written by Rob Branson, published by ZML Corp LLC.

This Page Intentionally Left Blank

About the Author

Hi my name is Rob Branson. I've been an author for many years now, and have quite a bit of experience in the industry. I got started selling eBooks on my own websites and then made my way into Amazon, selling Kindle, paperback, and audiobooks. I have made all the mistakes, done all the research, and spent all the time so you don't have to! This book will effortlessly guide you through the process of creating and publishing your Kindle and paperback book on Amazon. Once a book is published in KDP, it can be available for purchase on Amazon within 24 hours. If while reading this book you have any questions, feel free to e-mail me at rob@fastlink.xyz. Without further ado, let's create our book!

How to Publish a Book

Introduction

In the past when people talked about writing a book, others would think to themselves, "Good luck getting it published." Even after the internet went mainstream, it has still been a lengthy, expensive process. You had to write the draft, send it to the publisher who would then have to approve it. Then YOU had to order hundreds of copies of your own book, to the tune of thousands of dollars. And unless you were backed by a big publisher, you then had to market the book yourself. For most authors, the whole process turned into a money trap. It was incredibility costly, and if you couldn't market your book properly, you were left with boxes of whatever book you wrote sitting in your garage. But then came Amazon…

Amazon has changed the way average Joes are able to produce books. No longer does it take a huge down payment or a large publishing company to produce and market a book. Now, with just a laptop and the internet, you too can become an author. There is basically no overhead or upfront costs. This is huge! This has completely changed the playing field, and it's now easier than ever to get into the industry.

In this novel, we will be going over the publishing process for getting your book onto Amazon. I am going to assume you have either already written a book, or have a book in mind that you want to write, and now want to get it published. First, we will go over the program(s) needed to create your book. Then we'll go over creating a stunning cover to attract visitors and help your book sell. And last, we will go over the actual publishing process, making your book available in both Kindle and paperback form on Amazon, available for purchase.

The process of creating and uploading a Kindle book versus a paperback book is slightly different. For this reason, the first section of this novel will go over creating your Kindle book, and the second section will go over creating your paperback book. While you can create just one or the other, it's beneficial to have both versions on Amazon, as you are able to market your book to a larger audience.

Part 1A
Making Your Book

Creating Your Kindle Cover

The first thing you need to do is create a cover for your Kindle book. You have two options for this: do it yourself or hire someone to do it for you. If you decide to create the cover yourself, there is a wonderful website called Canva.com which, even for the artistically impaired, allows you to make stunning book covers. The website only charges to use their images, but at just $1 per image, it is quite reasonable. I've made quite a few covers on Canva and highly recommend it.

Your second option is to hire someone to make the cover for you. While this may have been expensive in the past, it's not anymore. One of my favorite websites to use is called Fiverr (shortened link to site: **fastlink.xyz/fiver**). Here you'll find hundreds of graphic designers willing to make you a book cover for as low as $5. Many of these designers are in foreign countries, however they still do great work. I've had quite a few covers designed on this website and for the most part, I've been impressed.

Just make sure you find someone with lots of quality reviews.

Whether you go with option A or B, know the standard dimensions for a Kindle book cover is 1600 pixels wide by 2560 pixels long.

Writing Your Kindle Book

If you're making both a Kindle and paperback book, the Kindle book should be made first, as it makes this whole process much easier. First you will need to download a program called "Kindle Create," which I have a shortened link to here: **fastlink.xyz/kindle**.

Kindle Create (KC) is a software made by Amazon meant specifically to create Kindle books. The software is rather restricted in terms of editing goes, however it's the best program to currently create a Kindle book because of how well it integrates into Amazon. Before KC came out, you had to make your book with Microsoft Word and upload it to Amazon. Amazon didn't recognize all the coding in Microsoft Word, so your finished book would have tons of spacing and margin issues. It made it look highly unprofessional which hurt customer feedback.

KC has changed this. When you make a book using KC, how it appears in the program is how it will appear on your customer's Kindle and eBook reader devices. I'll be going over how to make your book in KC however, I'd first like to go over some limitations of the program. This program is rather new, so I'm sure Amazon will continue expanding upon it in the future. However at this time, it's quite limited. Some of the limitations include:

- There are currently only three font choices
- No way to create bulleted or numbered lists
- Only accepts JPG images
- Only copying works in Kindle Create, not cutting
- No spelling/grammar check feature

Because of all these limitations, with the most concerning being the lack of a spelling/grammar check, I would suggest first writing your book in Microsoft Word (or Google docs) and then importing it over into Kindle Create.

While writing your book in Microsoft Word, you want to exclude pictures and the table of contents; these will be added in later in KC. Considering this, if you will be including pictures in your book, I would suggest putting a placeholder in Word where pictures will go. For example, you could write (picture-1) where you want your first image to appear. Then, when you go over the final touches in KC, you will know where to insert your images.

So let's say you have finished writing your book

in Microsoft Word. The first thing you want to do is separate chapters via "page breaks." This will allow KC to know where each chapter starts when you import it over. To do this, click "control + enter" on your keyboard at the end of each chapter. You can also view where page breaks are in Word by click the "show/hide" button at the top of the page (as shown in the photo below).

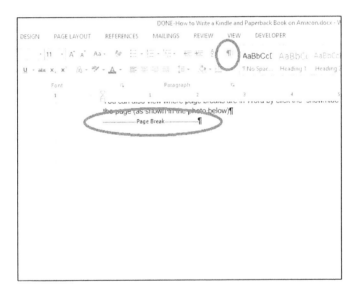

Next you will individually highlight each chapter title, and choose the "Heading 1" option in the styles tab. This allows Kindle Create to recognize each Chapter Title.

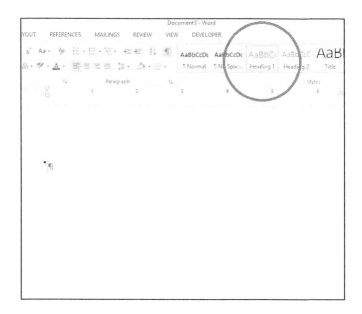

After this, you will edit the "Normal" style, which all your text should be associated with. To do this right click on "Normal," in the styles menu at the top. Then choose "Modify." Click the "Format" button in the button left corner, and choose "Paragraph." Make sure the spacing is set to 0pt for before and after. Set the line spacing to single. Then under the special drop down choose "first line," and increase it to 0.2." This will indent the first line of each paragraph, as customary in most books.

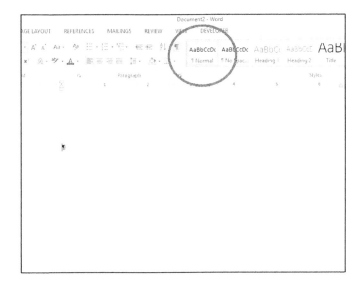

After this is all complete, now is a good time to do a spelling/grammar check on your Word document. This is important, because currently KC does not have a spell check feature. After you have performed a spell check, it is now time to import your word document into Kindle Create.

Part 1B
Kindle Create

We will start by importing our word document into Kindle Create. To do this, open KC and click "new project." Then find the saved Word document, and KC will import it for you. We will now put in our missing images, a table of contents, and style our book, putting the final touches on it before we upload it to Amazon.

Images

Now you can start putting any necessary images into your book. The image placeholders you positioned in Microsoft Word will be used as a guide for inserting your images. To insert images, right click on the location you want the image and click "insert." As mentioned, KC currently only accepts .JPG files, so you cannot bring in other types of image files such as .PNG. If you have an image you need to convert to JPG, the website **www.png2jpg.com** does this for free. The same website has sister sites which convert other picture formats to .JPG.

After each image is uploaded, you need to format it. This includes giving it a name and making sure it is size appropriate. First, click on the image, and you'll notice a box will appear in the top right corner labeled "alt text." This is a text box where you can label your image. This will be shown to readers when they click on the image in your book. You can make this a brief title of the image, or write out a whole description if you'd like.

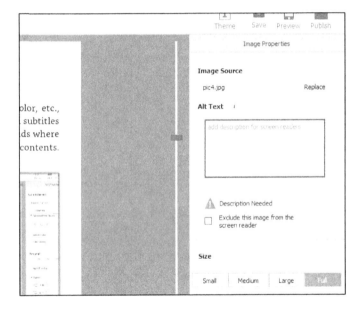

Next you want to figure out the size and position you want to make your image. You can place the image on the far right, far left, or center. You also have the option to make it small, medium, large or full. And with the "full" option, there is an option to keep the image within the margin or have it "bleed," which is where it extends to the very edge of the page. This is actually a good choice for large photos, as they then become a little bigger and easier to view for the reader. Know too, no matter the size you make your image, readers have the option to click on it and "zoom in," making it more visible.

Book and Chapter Titles

Before making edits such as font size, color, etc., you need to assign labels to chapter titles and subtitles throughout the book. This is so KC understands where pages are located in reference to the table of contents. We will start with the title page.

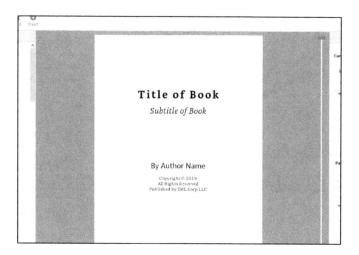

Highlight the title of your book and choose the "Book Title" button. This is located on the right side of the screen, under "elements." When you click the "Book Title" button, the style of your title will immediately change to the default KC title settings. Don't worry about this for right now as we will go over styling later; for right now we are just labeling. Next, you will continue this process with the book subtitle, as well as the author name. There are buttons for both of these also located on the right side of the screen in the "elements" section.

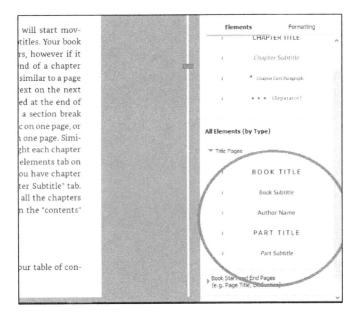

Once done with the title page, we will start moving down to the chapter titles and subtitles. Your book should already be broken into chapters, however if it isn't, you need to right click at the end of each chapter and choose "add section break." This is similar to a page break in Microsoft Word, and starts text on the next page. Section breaks will mostly be used at the end of chapters. You may also choose to use a section break when you want all text of a certain topic on one page, or you want a picture and text to all be on one page.

Similar to the book title, you want to highlight each chapter title and choose "Chapter Title" in the elements tab on the right side of the screen. Then if you have chapter subtitles, do the same with the "Chapter Subtitle" tab. Once this is complete, you should see all the chapters shown on the left side of the screen in the "contents" pane.

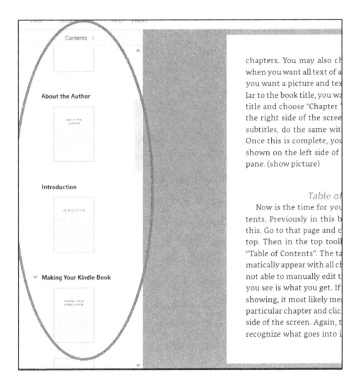

Table of Contents

After the title page and chapter titles have been labeled, it's now a good idea to create a table of contents (TOC). I would suggest placing the TOC right after the title page. To do this, click the "insert" button on the top left corner of the screen, and choose "Table of Contents." The table automatically grabs the titles from all your chapters, thus effectively making a TOC for you. If a certain chapter title is not showing, it most likely means you didn't highlight that particular chapter and click "Chapter Title" on the right side of the screen. Again, that is how the TOC is able to recognize what chapters are associated with your book.

If a title in the TOC is labeled incorrectly, you can change it by finding the chapter it correlates with on the left side of the screen, in the contents pane. Then make sure the title has the preferred text. Highlight the title and click the "Chapter Title" box on the right side of the screen in the "Elements" tab. Once you do this, it should update the title in the TOC.

Styling

Next we will be styling our eBook. The right side of the screen has all the editing capabilities available for you in the "formatting" tab.

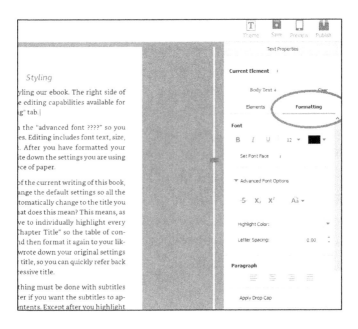

Make sure to open the "advanced font options," as well as click "set font face" so you can see all your choices. Editing includes font face, font size, spacing, indents, and paragraph orientation.

Unfortunately, as of the current writing of this book, there is no way to change the settings so all the titles in your book automatically change to a default format. So what does this mean? This means, as of right now, you have to individually highlight every chapter title, subtitle, and piece of body text and format them to your liking. For this reason, whatever choices you decide on for your titles, body text, etc., make sure to write them down in Notepad or on a piece of paper so you remember what they are.

Formatting text is an author preference; there is not a "standard" way to format text. You may find that the default text settings given by KC fit your book just fine, and you go with those. Whatever you choose, I do recommend indenting the first line of each paragraph, and setting the body text font size to 12.

Part 1C
Publishing Your Kindle Book

You have completed your book in Kindle Create, and you're ready to sell it on Amazon. While saving a book in KC puts it into a .KCB format, clicking the "publish" button puts it into the needed .KPF format so it's ready for upload to Amazon. So once you are finished editing your book in Kindle, save it, and then click the publish button in the upper right hand corner of the screen.

Next you're going to go to kdp.amazon.com. Here you'll login with the same username and password as your Amazon account. If this is your first time logging in, there may be some check boxes you have to agree to. Once you're in, in the top left of the screen under "Create a New Title," click Kindle eBook.

There are three pages associated with uploading your Kindle book to Amazon. The first page asks for details, such as the title and a description of your book. The second page has you upload your ebook manuscript and cover, and the third page goes over pricing. We will be going over each page separately, as they are all important.

Page 1 – Details

The first information asked for is the title and subtitle of your book. If you're writing something such as a fiction novel, then you can name it whatever you please. If you're writing a non-fiction book, such as one on teaching people how to lose weight, it's a little different. Amazon places a bit of importance on what is in the title and subtitle in the search results. Many times you will see books with very few reviews and sales, however they show up first in the results because the words you searched for matched their title. For this reason, I would recommend placing important words you think customers will be searching for into your title.

So let's say you're writing a book on how to lose weight. You could flat out name your book "how to lose weight" with some type of catchy subtitle. Or you could make up your own title, and then place the words "how to lose weight" somewhere in the subtitle.

E.X. Flab No More: How to Lose Weight Fast and Easy

Granted, this isn't the only criteria Amazon uses when determining search results, however it is one of them, so it is something to consider when naming your book.

Next you will put in the author's name. Many authors choose to use what is called a "pen name," which is basically a fake name you use to write your books. There are different reasons to do this, but it all boils down to a personal preference. Whatever name you choose will be put in this box. There is also an option to list contributors to your book, such as additional authors, editors, etc. if more than one person is associated with your book.

Next Amazon has you write out a description of your book. This is the text your audience views when on your Amazon book page. This is important, as many customers will read this section to learn more about your book, and it can make or break if they will buy it. Know that Amazon allows certain HTML elements in the description. You can use these elements to make your text stand out (bold font, larger font, bullet points, etc.). Here is a link to the approved HTML elements allowed in descriptions: **fastlink.xyz/html**.

HTML is a fairly easy coding language to learn. If you're unfamiliar with it, w3schools.com and codeacademy.com are two great, free resources to help you learn a little more about it.

After this, you are asked to place up to 7 keywords in the given boxes to help users find your book. Make sure to use all 7 boxes! This is another variable

Amazon uses to place your book in search results when customers search on their website. So these keywords are important to enter.

Next you want to choose the categories your book will be located in. You are allowed to place your book in up to two categories, so make sure to use both. A good idea is to find a similar book already on Amazon, and then examine what categories that book is in, and emulate it.

Page 2 – Content

On the second page you will upload your cover and eBook manuscript.

You will first upload the manuscript. Your Kindle book should be in the .KPF extension, which was done when we "published" our book using Kindle Create. Find this file and upload it here.

After uploading your book, you now have to upload your cover. Amazon only accepts .JPG or .TIFF images for your cover. As stated previously, the standard size for a cover is 1410 x 2250 pixels. You'll also see a "cover creator" option here. We will go over this more later, but don't use it! It's not good.

Page 3- Rights & Pricing

There are a few items which need to be addressed

on the "Rights & Pricing" page.

The first item is "KDP Select Enrollment." This relates to Amazon's "Kindle Unlimited" program, which is basically a streaming service for books. It appears that books are going the way of TV and movies, as in instead of buying books, many people are paying a monthly subscription fee and getting to read as many books as they like. Authors are then given a small stipend based on the number of pages of their book read by Kindle Unlimited customers. The amount paid to authors changes, but right now it comes out to about $5 per 1000 pages read on Amazon. This is something you will want to research yourself, and decide if you want your book enrolled in this program. Personally, I have some books enrolled and others I don't. It depends on the type of information I have in the book, and how much I think it's worth. If you have your book enrolled in KDP select, that book is exclusive to Amazon, meaning you cannot sell it in other marketplaces.

Next is "Territories." For most authors, you will leave the default box checked, which is "all territories." This just means your book can be sold worldwide on the various Amazon websites.

After that, comes the "Royalty and Pricing" section. There are two commission structures you can place your book into:

- **30% Commission** - Books can be priced between $0.99 - $200.
  E.X. You sell your book for $30. Amazon takes $20 and you receive $10.

- **70% Commission** - Books can be priced between $2.99 - $9.99.
  E.X. You sell your book for $5. Amazon takes $1.50 and you receive $3.50.

Unless you have a book that is highly valuable and you want to price very high, I would suggest placing your book into the 70% commission structure. This gives you the most profit for each sale, and it is where most authors in the Kindle store currently price their books. I would suggest looking at similar books in your category to determine a suitable price for your novel. Amazon has a "KDP price support" tool which provides you a suggested price to list your book. Supposedly this suggested price provides you with the best price to sales ratio, however I would take this "price support tool" with a grain of salt.

Next we have the "Matchbook" section. This only applies if you have both a Kindle and paperback version of your book available on Amazon. If a customer buys the paperback version of your book, they are given the option to buy the Kindle version for $2.99 or less, depending on what price you put here. I would enroll your Kindle book in Matchbook, and put a price of $0.99. For the most part, no one is going to buy your Kindle book if they already are buying the paperback version. However for $0.99, they sometimes do, and this adds a little extra money to your pocket.

Last we have "Book Lending." Checking this box allows customers who have bought your Kindle book the ability to lend it to another Amazon customer to read. While at first glance you may think this is silly, you are actually given a stipend each time your book is lent out to another customer. From my experience and research, it makes sense to enroll your book in the lending program.

You are now finished with all three sections of the uploading process. Click "publish your Kindle eBook" in the bottom right corner of the screen. Your book is then reviewed by Amazon, and will be available in the Kindle store within 72 hours.

As a **token of appreciation** to my readers, I am offering my special report above titled *Amazon Advertising Secrets* **absolutely free!** In this report, you'll learn a unique strategy you can use to advertise your books on Amazon, gaining additional sales! Just copy & paste the link below into your browser and put in your email address, and it will immediately be sent to you!

fastlink.xyz/secrets

Part 2A
Making Your Paperback Book

The process for making your paperback book is a bit different than the Kindle book. This guide will be going over how to make your paperback book in Microsoft Word. Other word processors will work, and you will most likely be able to apply what you learn in this book to other word processors, however Microsoft Word is the most common word processor so that's what I'll be using here. Recently Kindle Create has added the option to convert your Kindle book into a paperback version. Considering the editing abilities in KC are very limited and there is no spell check, I would advise against this. Microsoft Word is currently the best place to write your paperback book.

The first thing you should do is download a template for whatever size book you are making. Amazon allows the following sizes for books (inches, W x L):

- 5 x 8

- 5.25 x 8
- 5.5 x 8.5
- 6 x 9
- 5.06 x 7.81
- 6.14 x 9.21
- 6.69 x 9.61
- 7 x 10
- 7.44 x 9.69
- 7.5 x 9.25
- 8 x 10
- 8.5 x 11
- 8.27 x 11.69
- 8.25 x 6
- 8.25 x 8.25
- 8.5 x 8.5

For most author's first book, and especially if your book is less than 100 pages, I would stick with a 5" x 8" book. Amazon defaults the paperback book size to 6" x 9" (I'm not sure why, it's a little big). So when you go through the upload process, make sure to change this option if you want a different size. Also know whatever book size you choose cannot be changed later on. Once chosen, it's set in stone. The only way to change it would be to unpublish your paperback book and create a new one.

Once you decide on a paperback book size, Amazon has templates to be used with Microsoft

Word. These templates provide the correct margins for when Amazon prints the book at their warehouses. This is important, because if you just submitted a regular Microsoft Word document which was not formatted correctly, your book would come out extremely poor and unprofessional. This would gainer negative reviews and lose you customers. For this reason, you definitely want to use the correctly formatted template for whatever size book you choose. To obtain a paperback template from Amazon, go to the shortened link provided here: **fastlink.xyz/paperback**.

You have already created your Kindle book in Microsoft Word, so you can just copy and paste it into your paperback template. After copying the text over, I encourage you to use the styles tab in the top right corner which includes Normal, Heading 1, etc. This will help the table of contents you create later recognize each chapter. Also, it is easier to format text in your document, as all you have to do is highlight it, and then choose one of your ready-made styles from the top.

In the Styles tab, there is a style labeled "Normal," which will be the majority of the text in your paperback book. Two things I would recommend doing immediately within this "Normal" style are indenting the first line of each paragraph to 0.2" and justifying the font. For those unfamiliar, justified font is when the font stretches across the whole margin, as opposed to being left aligned. Almost all paperback books on the market use justified font, as it is easier on the reader. There are four alignment options (left, center, right, justify), with justified alignment being the one on the far right in Microsoft Word.

To change the "Normal" style, right click on it in the Styles tab and then choose modify. First, change the alignment to justified. Then at the bottom choose "format," and click paragraph. In paragraph, under "special," choose "first line" and make this 0.2." You can use this same method to change the other styles (Heading 1, Title, etc.) in your Styles menu.

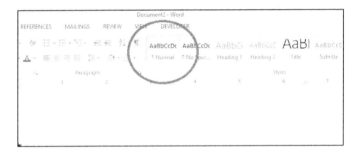

Considering we left out images in the Kindle Word document, we will now be inserting those missing images into the paperback version. To insert an image, click the "Insert" tab at the top, and then click "Pictures." I would suggest making the image the entire width of the text, within the given margins. Do not bring the image outside of the margins or you risk losing parts of it in the page bounding (this rule does not apply to those with full page bleed pictures, which we'll touch on later).

Once you have your book laid out correctly, and everything appears to your liking, it's time to put in the table of contents. To do this click the "References" tab, then choose "Table of Contents." Once this is completed, use the spell check tool located in Word. You want to make sure there are no spelling or grammar errors. Once complete, you want to proof read your entire book. Even read it out loud if you want to. While you may be different, I've caught errors in the second or even third time proofreading my book. Spelling errors, run on sentences, or any other "unprofessional" errors can hurt how your book appears to customers and negatively affect reviews.

When you have proof-read your book and everything is completely finished, click "save as." Then from the "save as type" dropdown, save your document as a PDF file. This will be used when we upload our book to Amazon later.

When saving as a PDF, two buttons pop up which are next to "optimize for." The default button checked is "minimum size." You *do not* want this option checked. Make sure to choose the button above it which reads "standard." This is important, as if you don't choose the standard setting, any photos in your book will be saved in a low quality format making them grainy in the final paperback book.

Paperback Cover

The paperback cover is a little different from the Kindle cover due to how it's uploaded. Amazon currently accepts paperback covers in a PDF format, or a .PNG or .JPG format. If you're using a .JPG or .PNG picture though, you have to use something called "Cover Creator." We will touch on this a little later.

You have already made the front cover, but now a back cover has to be made. Some author just fill in the back cover with a solid color. Others will put text on the back cover, which either has quotes or gives a summary of the book. This is personal preference, but you do need something on the back of the book, even if it's just a solid color. Make it the same size as the front cover (1600 x 2560 pixels). Be aware the bottom right corner of the back cover will be covered by a barcode.

Amazon has a page which allows you to download blank paperback cover templates. These templates are used as a guide to place your front and back cover into. To download a template, go to this shortened link here: **fastlink.xyz/cover**. The templates are different sizes depending on the number of pages in your book, so make sure to put in the correct number. This can be gathered from your Microsoft Word document. I have an example of what a template looks like on the next page.

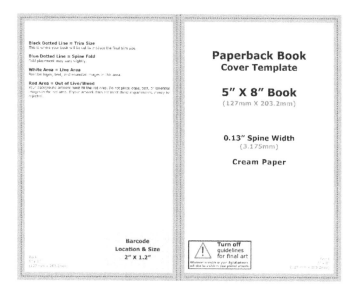

Next you have to take your front and back cover images and combine them onto this template. This part takes a little bit of Photoshop or Paint.net work. Photoshop costs money, however Paint.net is a free program very similar to Photoshop, which is used for editing images. You can download it at the link here: **fastlink.xyz/paint**.

If you're not very computer savvy, or don't feel comfortable with this process, you can hire someone from Fiverr (**fastlink.xyz/fiver**) to do this for you for $5. Just make sure to give them your front and back cover, as well as the template you downloaded.

If you look at the template, you'll see a red

rectangle around the edge of the book, as well as a black dotted line. No text can be touching the red rectangle, and the book gets cut where the black dotted line is. This is important to know if you decide to create your own cover.

I have to mention that Amazon has a "cover designer" on their backend which can be used for the Kindle and paperback cover, however it is quite poor. The covers come out looking like a 1st grader designed them, just because of how primitive of a software it is (and not an artistic 1st grader either). So while it may be tempting to use it because of the ease of the process, I would highly discourage you from doing this. A cover is a very important part of the selling process, and a bad one can turn customers away. At $5 for a cover on Fiverr, there's no reason not to have a quality cover.

Part 2B
Publishing Your Paperback Book

The process of uploading your paperback book to Amazon is similar to the Kindle book. First, go to kdp.amazon.com. Then find your already uploaded Kindle book and click "create paperback" below it. If you are not making a Kindle book and strictly making a paperback book, you can click the "Paperback" button under "Create New Title" in the top left corner of the screen.

Page 1- Paperback Details

If you're linking your Paperback and Kindle book, make sure they have the same exact title and subtitle. Amazon makes a big deal about this and for obvious reasons. The title should auto populate from your Kindle book, so this shouldn't be too much of an issue.

Similar to the Kindle book, you will then put in your description, seven keywords, as well as choose two categories to place your book into. I would just copy everything over from the Kindle version for all these variables, as you are uploading the same exact book here, just in a different format.

Page 2- Paperback Content

All paperback books are required to have an ISBN. If you look online, buying an ISBN can cost hundreds of dollars. Luckily, Amazon is gracious enough to give you one completely free. Click the "assign me a free KDP ISBN" button, and one will be generated for you instantaneously.

Next you have print options (PO). These are the options which pertain to how your book is printed at the Amazon warehouses.

The first PO section is "Interior & Paper Type." Your choices include:

- Black & white interior with cream paper
- Black & white interior with white paper
- Color interior with white paper

The color interior option costs a little more to print, which means you would have to charge more for your book. So unless you have a book with in depth pictures which you need to appear in color, I would choose the default option, "cream with black text."

The second PO section is trim size. As stated before, Amazon defaults to 6 x 9. For some authors this may be fine. For the most part though, books under 100 pages are best with the smaller 5 x 8 template. The template size you used to create your book will determine what option you choose here.

The third PO section is "Bleed Settings." There are two choices here: no bleed or bleed. This refers to the interior of the book, and if you want the pictures and text within the margins, or to "bleed" to the edges. Usually you'll see children's books with page bleed, with an example being The Cat in the Hat. The illustrations in the book go right to the edges. So unless you are writing a children's book or know specifically you want page bleed, you should choose the "no bleed" choice here.

The fourth PO section is the "Paperback Cover Finish." Your two choices here are: matte or glossy. For most books, I would recommend a glossy finish as this looks more professional. This is a personal preference, however most paperback books on the market do have a glossy finish.

Next you will upload your actual paperback manuscript. Click the "upload" button, and choose the PDF file we had saved previously.

After this, you will upload your cover. Here you have two options: you can upload a PDF version of your cover or click "Cover Creator," and upload a JPG or PNG version of your cover into Amazon's cover software. If you're having someone make your cover for you, you should advise them to make it into a PDF. This makes this process much easier.

If you only have a JPG or PNG file, you can choose Cover Creator (CC). When using CC, there are a variety of cover options to choose from. Make sure to choose the one shows the full picture, with your front cover on the right and back cover on the left. They'll be a few different text boxes on top of the picture. Delete all the wording out of them, as this will make them go away. I have an example below of what your book cover should look like once it is uploaded properly in CC.

As you can see, the images associated with the cover go to the edges. All text is located within the interior red line, and the book will be cut at the exterior dotted black line. If you try to send a cover through that breaks these rules, Amazon may not accept it and you have to start the process over again. Once done, click save. It will take you back to page 2 of the upload process.

Once both the cover and manuscript have been uploaded, you will now click the "launch previewer" button at the very bottom of the page. The load time here can take a little bit, sometimes 10 minutes or longer before your book is available to preview. Once loaded, I highly encourage you to go through each page of your uploaded book and verify everything looks correct. How it looks in this previewer will be how it is printed. If anything looks off, click the back button and correct the error in your Microsoft Word document. Then again, save it as a PDF and re-upload your book.

After you have reviewed your book and verified it looks correct, click the "save and continue" button, which will bring you to page 3.

Page 3- Paperback Rights & Pricing

Pricing is a little different with the paperback book due to the printing cost, as well as a 60% commission payout versus 70%. Many authors charge a little bit more for their paperback book in order to factor in these costs. A good idea is to price it so you will receive the same commission payout with both the paperback and Kindle book.

<u>Example</u>

- Kindle Book priced at $5.00 - 30% (Amazon fee) = $3.50 commission paid
- Paperback Book priced at $10.00 - 40% (Amazon Fee) - $2.15 (Printing Cost) = $3.85 commission paid

Amazon shows you all the fees automatically when you type in your price, and calculates what you will earn.

There is an option with paperback books to allow "Expanded Distribution." This places your book in sister stores of Amazon, however the commission per sale is only 40%, as opposed to 60% with Amazon. You'll get more sales, however you'll make less. This is something you'll want to decide on your own if it's worth it for your book.

Before publishing your paperback book, Amazon has an option which allows a finished version to be sent to your house. This is so you can inspect it before it goes on the market. If this the first paperback book you are making, I highly suggest paying the $2.15 to get this "proof copy," waiting till it arrives at your house, and then inspecting it before you click that publish button. All the previous information you entered will be saved, meaning if everything looks okay when you receive the book, you simply click the "publish" button; you do not have to re-enter any information.

Once you hit the "publish" button, your book will be available for purchase on Amazon within 72 hours. If there is some type of error in your book (text outside margins, cover image violates guidelines, etc.), Amazon will contact you within this time period and ask you to fix the error. At which point you can fix it, and then re-upload it to Amazon to have it reviewed again.

Part 3
Linking the Kindle and Paperback Book

As long as the titles to both versions of your book match correctly, they should link automatically once they are both uploaded to Amazon. If 72 hours *after* your paperback book appears on Amazon it is still not linked to your Kindle book, you can send Amazon an email and they will do it manually for you.

To do this, login to your KDP account. Then click "help" in the upper right hand corner. Then click "contact us" in the lower left hand corner. There is an option you can choose which relates to linking Kindle and paperback books. Make sure to include the title, the author name, and the ASIN #'s of both books in your email, as this will allow for quicker processing for the Amazon team.

Conclusion

Well there you have it, you have successfully made a Kindle and paperback book and uploaded them to Amazon. I hope I was able to successfully guide you through this process, providing you with the confidence and know-how to publish your book. If you have any questions, you're welcome to message me at rob@fastlink.xyz. Good luck in your writing endeavors!

If you enjoyed this book, you may also like:

How to Make an Audiobook
Create, Narrate, & Record Your Own Audiobook Using Audacity

Shortened Link to Amazon Page:
fastlink.xyz/audiobook

Want to earn extra income from your books? This can be done by making an audiobook! In this book Rob Branson shows you everything you need to know, from start to finish, on how to make an audiobook. Look professional and stand out from your competition. Learn how to make an audiobook now!

The Crash Signal
The One Signal That Predicts a Stock Market Crash

Shortened Link to Amazon Page:
fastlink.xyz/crash

If you know anything about the stock market, you know crashes are inevitable… but losing money in those crashing doesn't have to be! In this book, Tim Morris shows you the one signal which has flashed before every stock market crash for the last 60 years! Will you be prepared for the next crash? Save your money before it's too late with The Crash Signal!

Make Money Online
Your Guide on How to Get Rich With Information Products

Shortened Link to Amazon Page:
fastlink.xyz/make

Rob Branson shows you the secrets the top gurus in the field have been using for years to acquire wealth online. Tim holds nothing back & provides you with all the secrets that you too can use to become rich using the internet. Whether you want to make a little money on the side or start a full time business, it all can be done with the strategies provided in this book!

Printed in Great Britain
by Amazon